THE TEACHER'S BIG BOOK OF FUN

Arnold Kanter and Wendy Kanter
Illustrated by Tony Tallarico

CONTEMPORARY BOOKS
A TRIBUNE COMPANY

Library of Congress Cataloging-in-Publication Data

Kanter, Arnold B., 1942–
    The teacher's big book of fun / Arnold Kanter and Wendy Kanter;
illustrated by Tony Tallarico.
       p.   cm.
    ISBN 0-8092-3161-1
    1. Teaching—Humor.   I. Kanter, Wendy.   II. Title.
LB1027.K267   1996
371.3'0207—dc20

96-15158
CIP

Painting on page 20: *La Gioconda* (Mona Lisa). Ca. 1503–06. Louvre, Paris, France. Photo by Giraudon/Art Resource. New York.

Published by Contemporary Books
An imprint of NTC/Contemporary Publishing Company
Two Prudential Plaza, Chicago, Illinois 60601-6790
Manufactured in the United States of America
International Standard Book Number: 0-8092-3161-1
10   9   8   7   6   5   4   3   2   1

To Leslie, for teaching me how to teach.

Wendy Kanter

To Mrs. Cushing, my fourth-grade teacher, who made me sit under the table in the front of the room because I hit Jimmy Slaughterman in the back of the head with a Spanish peanut while he was reading aloud to the class (it was worth it).

Arnie Kanter

To Mrs. Dunkin and Mrs. Tobin, my kindergarten and fifth-grade teachers, who taught me all I know (also to a hundred others).

Tony Tallarico

CONTENTS

INTRODUCTION

Searching for a useful book to write on problems in the teaching profession, we used our $2 million grant from the National Education Association to conduct a highly scientific worldwide survey of 8,622,433 teachers. We asked all of them one question: "Which of the following is the primary reason why teaching is not all that much fun anymore?"

a. ungrateful parents
b. meddling administrators
c. mischievous students
d. crabby colleagues
e. paltry pecuniary rewards
f. lack of a *Teacher's Big Book of Fun*

At long last we are free to publish our results:

Highly Scientific Survey Results

a. ungrateful parents 2
b. meddling administrators 6
c. mischievous students 3
d. crabby colleagues 8
e. paltry pecuniary rewards 14
f. lack of a *Teacher's Big Book of Fun* 8,622,000
g. none of the above 400

So, we figure we've got a blockbuster bestseller on our hands here. Will this funbook make you ecstatic? Content in your teaching and personal life? C'mon now, for a few bucks you want what thousands of dollars and years of therapy won't get you either? Be realistic. Would you settle for a chuckle or two, a momentary uptick in your disposition? Good. We've got a deal; let's go.

HOW THIS BOOK IS ORGANIZED

Randomly.

Look, we know you're a teacher. We know you expect a teacher's guide explaining how the book is organized, instructions on how to use the book, an index, and a bibliography. But hey, c'mon, this is a *funbook*. Lighten up a little. . . .

There, that's much better.

CONFIDENCE BUILDERS

Teaching is a tough business—we know. The pay is lousy, the students don't treat you with the respect you deserve, the time pressures are tremendous, and you're constantly being criticized by students, administrators, fellow teachers, and parents.

So in a profession like teaching, you need your confidence boosted once in a while. Relax, help is at hand. When you feel the need, turn to one of the Confidence Builders in this book, marked thusly:

If you have trouble with these Confidence Builders, watch for our next book, *The Teacher's Remedial Big Book of Fun*.

NAME THAT KID

To be a really good teacher, you've got to be able to remember the names of your students. Look at the picture on this page, memorize the names, and then turn the page to see if you can call your students by their correct names.

ORDER IN THE CLASS

Discipline is important. Without it, your classroom may become a shambles. With it, your classroom may become a shambles too, but at least you'll have had the satisfaction of a little revenge. Little Eddie Frankel has just dipped Suzy Stemple's pigtail in red paint. Choose the appropriate punishment for Eddie.

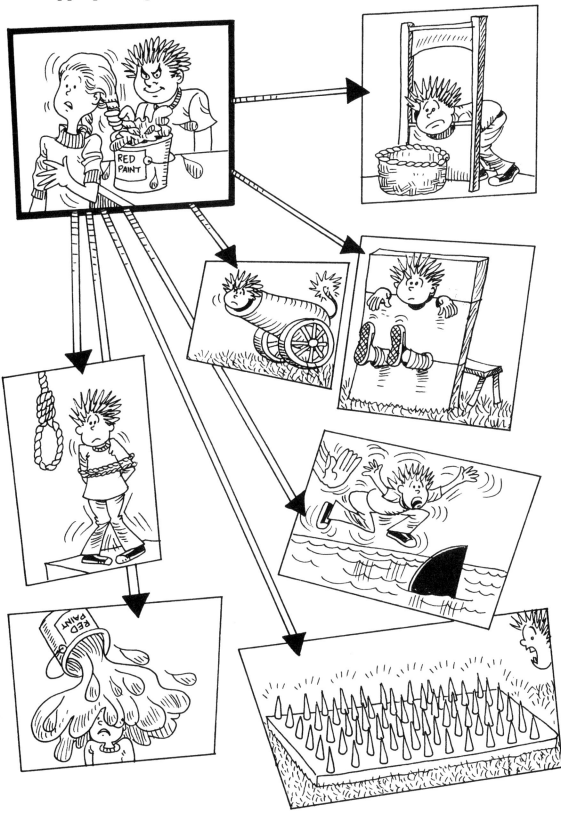

WHERE'S THAT COUNTRY?

Geography is an important subject for your students to learn. In order to help them, though, you've got to know a bit of geography yourself. Please paste the names of the countries in the proper places on this map.

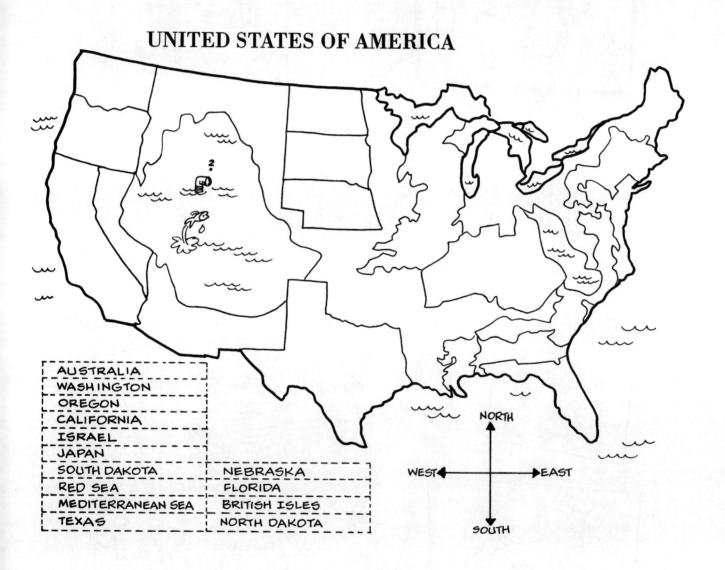

UNITED STATES OF AMERICA

AUSTRALIA
WASHINGTON
OREGON
CALIFORNIA
ISRAEL
JAPAN
SOUTH DAKOTA   NEBRASKA
RED SEA   FLORIDA
MEDITERRANEAN SEA   BRITISH ISLES
TEXAS   NORTH DAKOTA

NORTH
WEST   EAST
SOUTH

[Answer: Wait a minute—we think something got goofed up.]

6

PARENT-CHILD MATCHING

When parents come to school to pick up their children, it's impressive if you can identify which child a parent belongs to. Fortunately, parents often resemble their kids (or maybe it's the other way around). See if you can match the parents pictured below with their children.

RECESSING

Recess is a time for children to unwind. Still, it's your responsibility to make sure that they don't hurt themselves too badly. Which of the children in this picture could use a little closer supervision?

[Answer: Hey, they're just having a little fun.]

8

WHO DONE IT?

Sally Honst is a substitute teacher. Some of the students in her class have decided to play jokes on her. How many can you identify and stop before they create too much mischief?

9

FACULTY MEETING

The teachers of Greely Middle School are having a faculty meeting. Which teachers do you think are interested in what is being discussed?

BLACKBOARD ACROBATICS

It is difficult to write on a blackboard in a way that permits students to read what you are writing. Which of the teachers pictured below are doing a good job? What can you learn from their techniques?

MISSING HORMONES

As students move into adolescence, teachers must expect to see their hormones (the students') become more active. A good teacher will pick up subtle signs of this at early stages and take appropriate action. See if you can identify which students are reaching sexual awareness.

RELIGIOUS FERVOR

Though the United States Supreme Court has outlawed school prayer, some kids will still try to sneak it in. See if you can find the three trouble-making religious zealots in the picture so that you can punish them.

BODY PARTS

With the extent of unwanted pregnancy in high schools around the country, sex education has become even more important. Brush up on some key body parts by taking this matching test.

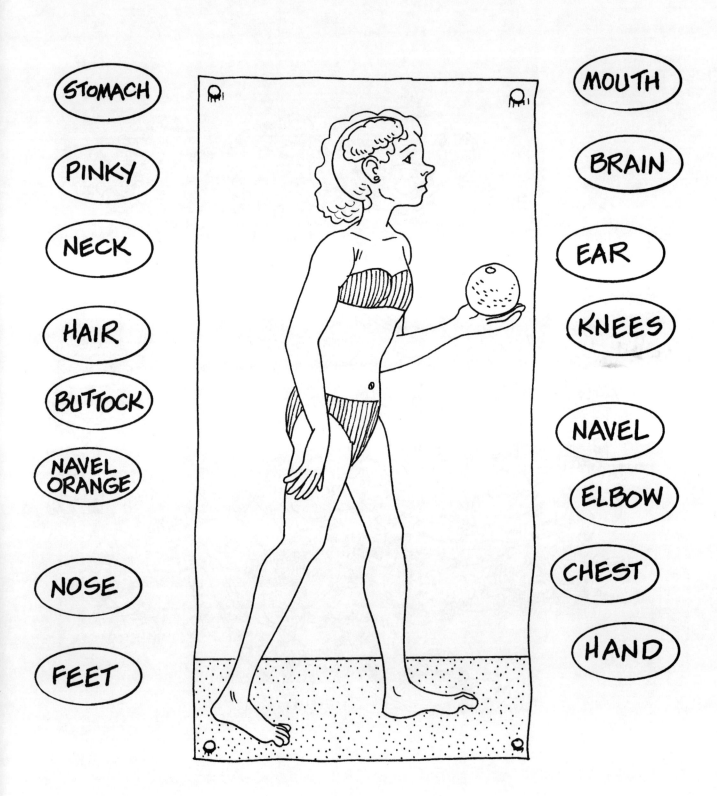

STOMACH

PINKY

NECK

HAIR

BUTTOCK

NAVEL ORANGE

NOSE

FEET

MOUTH

BRAIN

EAR

KNEES

NAVEL

ELBOW

CHEST

HAND

STACKING THE BOOKS

The books on the library shelves should be in alphabetical order, by author's last name. The children have used the library during study hour and mixed things all up. You have already alphabetized the bookshelf on the left. Good going. Now, just finish the job. Tidy things up by drawing arrows to put the books in their correct order.

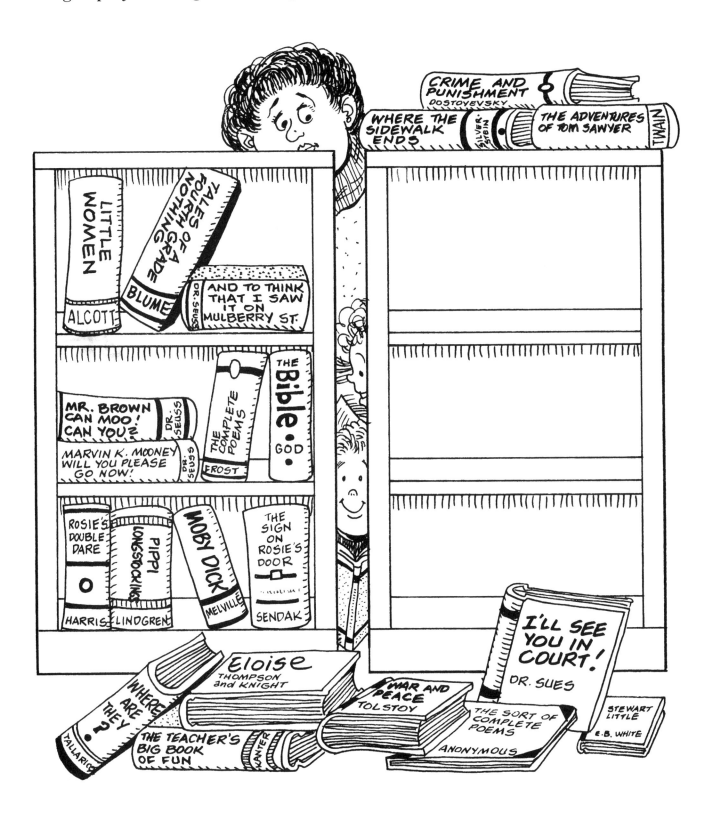

PLEDGE OF ALLEGIANCE

Nobody really knows the pledge of allegiance that well. Holly Higgins has just recited it. Please correct Holly.

ZOO TRIP

Miss Glass has taken her third-grade class on a field trip to the zoo. Fifteen of the children have strayed from the group. Can you help find the Glass class?

SCIENCE FAIR

The Nathan Hale Elementary School Science Fair is being held this week. The children are all very proud of their projects. Can you select the winner?

[Answer: Kid with the potato plant. His parents are the judges.]

PARENT CONFERENCES

These parents have just emerged from their midsemester meeting with their children's teacher. Can you guess which of them have received good news?

DRAWING IT OUT

Not all children have equal talent in drawing. But it's your job, as teacher, to encourage all of them. Which of the following comments would you make to the students who drew these pictures?

1. "I love your tree, Billy. Or is it a spider?"
2. "You seem to be a very talented abstract artist, Helen."
3. "That's a very nice house with legs, Suzy."
4. "That's a rather good likeness of the Mona Lisa."
5. "Is that your mommy or your daddy you drew, Philip?"

a.

d.

b.

c.

e.

20

HISTORICAL FIGURES

Somebody once said, "If you don't study history, you're doomed to repeat it." Somebody else once said, "History is often found in the past." And lots of other people have said other things about history also. Try to match the historical pictures with the captions.

1. Washington Crossing the Delaware
2. Washington Chopping Down the Cherry Tree
3. Washington Not Telling a Lie
4. Washington at a Fast-Food Restaurant
5. Washington Being the Father of Our Country

[Answers: 1. d; 2. a; 3. b; 4. c; 5. e]

KNOWING YOUR STUDENTS

While it's important not to prejudge children, you don't have to be an idiot about it. Remember that although appearances can be deceiving, usually they aren't. Which of the following children do you think will be a serious student? an outstanding athlete? a teacher's pet? a juvenile delinquent?

POLICE RAID

Local police have raided a suspected terrorist hideout, and teachers at Chester A. Arthur High have conducted a surprise inspection of the students' lockers. Unfortunately, the findings of the two searches have been mingled. Can you identify what came from Arthur High?

[Answer: They all came from Arthur High.]

23

SCHOOL SONG

Spirit at your school is lagging, and the principal has suggested that what you really need is a new school song. Compose a school song, chock-full of school spirit, using the following words:

Fight, fight, fight for dear old _____
We'll always be true to you, dear old _____
We're loyal as hell to dear old _____
Forever we'll love you, dear old _____
Oompah, oompah, oompah, oompah
Knock the other team on the head for dear old _____
Go Coyotes, go Coyotes, go Coyotes, go
Alma mater, alma mater, dear old _____

WHO MADE THE LUNCH?

It used to be that mothers made children's lunches for them, but in this day and age, many fathers perform that role as well. Can you identify which of these lunches were made by mommies and which by daddies?

25

DRESSING FOR SCHOOL

As a teacher, you have to set a good example for your students in the way you dress. Which of the following outfits would be appropriate for classroom wear?

[Answer: What's wrong with what they're wearing now?]

26

PENMANSHIP

Sloppy penpersonship can stunt a kid's growth. While it may be easy for you to make letters (because you've been doing it since you were a kid), it's not so darn easy for your students to learn to write a strange language. To get a feel for what they are going through, copy these letters from other alphabets.

COPY LETTERS ON WALL

AMERICAN GRAFFITT

	COPY LETTERS HERE
CHINESE	
FROM EASTER ISLAND	COPY LETTERS HERE

	COPY LETTERS HERE		COPY LETTERS HERE
RUSSIAN		BURMESE	
HEBREW	COPY LETTERS HERE	SANSKRIT	COPY LETTERS HERE

27

STORYTELLING

A good way to quiet down your class is to tell them a story. Make up a story using the following characters and elements:

a wicked, wicked witch
a pharmacist named Ralph
magic earmuffs
a dragon with three heads and fire coming out of its mouths
a goldfish named Orangespot
a pen that writes by itself
a stepmother named Lola
a stepfather named Orangespot

28

SCISSORS SKILL

You need to be able to handle scissors with ease in order to stay a step ahead of your students. Test your scissors dexterity by cutting out the form below.

GRADUATION SPEECH

Graduation is a significant milestone for your students. You have just been asked to deliver a speech to the graduating class of Getting Smart Elementary. Compose your speech using the following phrases:

SHORT OF FUNDS

You have to learn to make do with what you have as a teacher. Shantytown Elementary has been hit by a funding crisis, while Welltodo Prep has loads of funds. Can you tell which classroom is from which school?

CLASS PICTURE

Each year parents shell out millions of dollars for class pictures with their children in them. Mr. and Mrs. Hiram Oats want to find their little girl, Emily; and Mr. and Mrs. Ethel Hay want to find their little boy, Oscar, in their class picture. Can you help them locate their children?

[Answer: Emily was sick the day the picture was taken; Oscar cut school that day.]

HEAD COACH

You are football coach for Central High. Your team, the Newts, is playing the fearsome South High Monsters in the championship game this week. Because South is favored by seventy-six points, you are going to have to come up with some pretty tricky plays if the Newts are to pull this one out. Which of the following plays is likely to work?

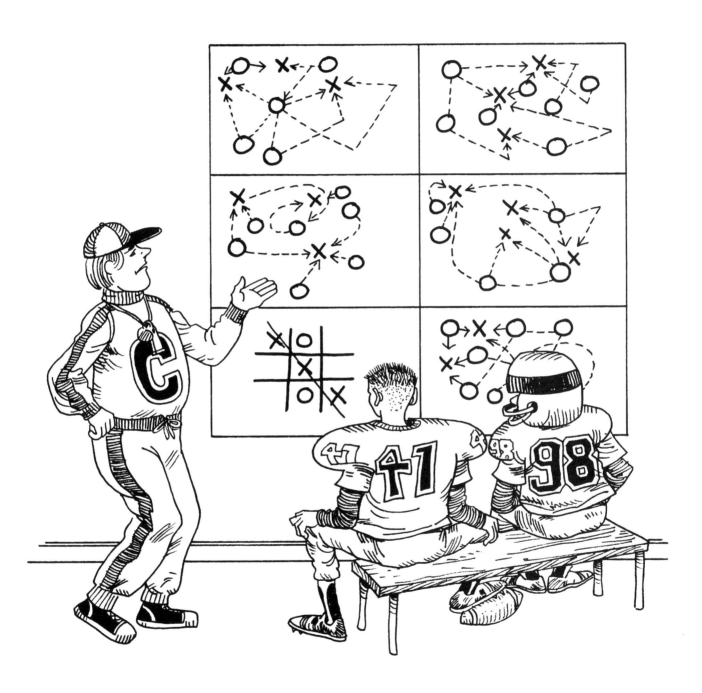

[Answer: None of them; you're going to get clobbered.]

YEARBOOK

The students of Endhere High School have just sent their school yearbook to press. They've selected the winning classmates in several categories. See if you can figure out who won which award.

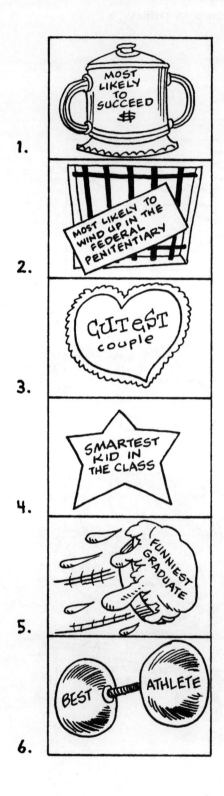

ORCHESTRA PRACTICE

The music teacher is ill today, and you've been asked to substitute as conductor of the orchestra. All of the students have taken their chairs, but some of them seem to be slightly out of place. Can you identify which children don't belong in the orchestra?

GETTING HEIGHT RIGHT

You have asked the children in your class to form a line, with the shortest person at the front and the tallest at the rear, so that they can walk down the hall to their next class. As you can see, they have not exactly followed your instructions. What is the fewest number of moves you can make to get the children ready to march down the hall?

[Answer: Who cares whether they line up by height, anyway?]

STUDENT CAFETERIA

Your school cafeteria subsidizes teacher lunches and prides itself on its fine selection. Which of the following lunches is available at your cafeteria?

[Answer: The frankfurter, but we're out of catsup, mustard, and pickles.]

STEPPING OUT

The students in Eastwood High's woodworking class have taken advantage of Mr. Gretsly's having stepped outside for a few minutes. See if you can identify some things that Mr. Gretsly is not going to be too pleased about upon his return.

FIND THE BEAR

The seventh-grade class at Smarten Up Junior High is on a nature retreat for the weekend. What they don't know is that there's a great big bear in the woods waiting to eat them up. If you can find the bear, you might be able to save them! (On the other hand, this is one of the hard facts about nature.)

GETTING FROM A TO Z

Mrs. Board is on the Alphabet Committee. She is on a very important mission. She must find all the letters of the alphabet, from A to Z, hidden throughout the city. Maybe you can help Mrs. Board. She certainly would appreciate it.

MATCHING OBSERVATIONS TO REPORTS

Part of being a teacher is knowing how to communicate your observations to parents. Match the observations listed in the left column to the proper report in the right column.

1. completely out of control

2. hits, bites, yanks, punches, pokes, slaps, grabs

3. smart-ass

4. doesn't shut up

5. liar

6. cry-baby

7. thief

8. faculty kid

a. a real free spirit

b. sensitive

c. has a remarkable imagination

d. active

e. a delight to have in class

f. has good hand-eye coordination

g. highly verbal

h. a bit aggressive

AVOID THE INTRUDER

If you're going to get any work done as a teacher, you have to be able to dodge all the people and things that are gonna want to try and get in your way. Can you help George B. Luck stick to his agenda as he walks (quickly) through the school? His work depends on it.

AUTOGRAPH HOUNDS

It's the end of the year, and the students at Notsohot High have circulated autograph books among their friends. Unfortunately, the pages have come loose from the books of Anne Antworthy, salutatorian of the class, and Zeke Zontner, the class dolt. See if you can return the proper pages to Anne and Zeke.

HOOPING IT UP

Five students in your senior calculus class have started to leave early because they say that they have to get to basketball practice. Can you identify which of them is not telling the truth?

44

FLUNKING FOR FUN

Flunking students is difficult. Nobody likes to tell kids that they've failed. But sometimes you have to bite the bullet. In addition to biting the bullet, you also sometimes have to flunk students. Studies show that the more you flunk students, the easier it gets. Practice flunking students by marking an *F* for all students in the following grading report.

SOPHOMORE ADVANCED PLACEMENT ENGLISH	
STEPHEN ANDERSOOT	
ANNE ARBOR	
LYNN BERGER	
AIDA BIGLUNCHE	
MAE BUSCHE	
REX FREXZEXTEX	
THOMAS GOOFINOFF	
M.T. HAID	
JAY LETTERMEN	
JOHN JOHN MECELI	
PASQUALLE C.O.D.	
STEW PIDD	
HARPO REELYWILDERDOFF	
MARIA REYES	
BARBARA SOLE	

HIGHLY RECOMMENDED

As a high school teacher you will be called upon to write recommendations for a lot of your students' college applications. Obviously, not all of them are students you'd really like to recommend. The trick is to write your letter so as to maintain your integrity without torpedoing the students' chances for admission. Practice writing a letter of recommendation using the following phrases:

HIGH HOPES HIGH
5 NOWAY DRIVE • GIVEUP, OREGON

better than average
shows real promise
has improved a bit lately
is generally pretty honest
rather well-liked by some of his
   best friends
not a major behavior problem

PICTURE I.D.

Let's face it, no matter how many times you tell your students to put their names on their artwork, there will always be a handful who forget. Can you return the work on the left to the right kids? Use the pictures on the right to help you.

[Answer: Your guess is as good as ours. The students don't remember, although Frank has a feeling they're all his.]

THE GRADING TARGET

Grading isn't easy. It's nearly impossible to be objective. For help in making those tough decisions, tack this page up in the faculty lounge. Then have one of your colleagues blindfold you and spin you around. Throw a dart at the target and follow the advice you get.

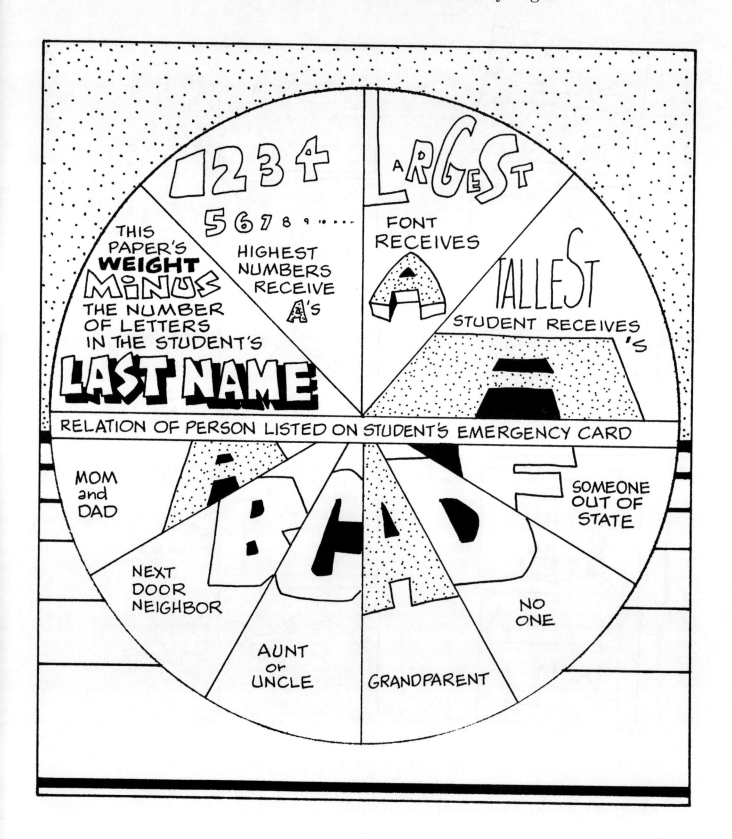

CONFERENCE OPENERS

It's sometimes nice to open a conference with a sample of your students' writing. If your students are using invented spelling, it's also nice to have some idea what they've written down so you can translate it for the parents. Match the invented spelling on the left to the standard spelling on the right.

1. XCPBLMARKKI.

2. T DG S MN.

3. I M U SBR HRO.

4. TS S U RNBO.

5. THIS IS ME PUTTING ON MY NEW BROWN SHOES.

a. My teacher's #1.

b. That teacher of mine really knows what she's talking about.

c. Listen up, Ma and Pa.

d. Take some advice from my teach.

e. I'm a real headache, it's true.

[Answers: 1. d; 2. e; 3. b; 4. a; 5. c]

49

PICTURE THIS

You've just returned from winter break. You need some impressive pictures to show your fellow teachers and to pass around the office. Just paste in photos from magazines or your family album as indicated.

PASTE PHOTO OF
YOUR FACE HERE

PASTE PHOTO
OF YOUR FACE
HERE

TO CATCH A CHEAT

Which of these excerpts from a senior high school English class may include some plagiarism?

a. Tha book we read was real good. I never read anything so good before.

b. This book makes me ask myself whether 'tis nobler in the mind to suffer the slings and arrows of outrageous fortune, or to take arms against a sea of troubles, and by opposing, end them. To die, to sleep—no more, and by a sleep to say we end the heartache and the thousand natural shocks that flesh is heir to; 'tis a consummation devoutly to be wish'd. To die, to sleep—to sleep, perchance to dream—ay, there's the rub, for in that sleep of death what dreams may come, when we have shuffled off this mortal coil, must give us pause; there's the respect that makes calamity of so long life: for who would bear the whips and scorns of time, th' oppressor's wrong, the proud man's contumely, the pangs of despis'd love, the law's delay, the insolence of office, and the spurns that patient merit of th' unworthy takes, when he himself might his quietus make with a bare bodkin who would fardels bear to grunt and sweat under a weary life.

c. This was a particularly thought-provoking book. I went fishing once too. I had a hard time catching fish too.

d. Sure were a lot of words.

HOUR POWER

It takes a whole lot of time to be a good teacher, often more time than any one person really has. Look at Betty's schedule and cross out the things she doesn't absolutely have to do today.

7:30 A.M. –8 A.M.	DISPLAY STUDENTS' DIORAMAS OF IROQUOIS OUTSIDE CLASSROOM
3:30 P.M. –5 P.M.	FACULTY MEETING
5 P.M. – 9:30 P.M.	EFFICIENT TEACHER'S MEETING
7 P.M. –9 P.M.	CHAPERONE 7TH –8TH GRADE DANCE
9:30 P.M. –10:30 P.M.	CALL MY 25 PEOPLE ON PHONE TREE TO REMIND THEM OF ALL-SCHOOL BAKE SALE
10:30 P.M. –12:30 A.M.	GRADE STUDENTS' REPORTS ON IROQUOIS
12:30 A.M. –1:30 A.M.	PREPARE QUIZ ON IROQUOIS

[Answer: Except for the faculty meeting and the dance, Betty's schedule is wide open.]

ANALOGIES

If you're gonna get your students ready to take the SATs, you better make sure you have the idea yourself. Try these analogy questions for practice.

1. status:teacher
   a. status:doctor
   b. status:rodent
   c. paper clip:White-Out
   d. mama chimp:baby chimp

2. teacher:salary
   a. something:nothing
   b. king:pellets
   c. The Old Man:Sea
   d. watermelon:spit

3. student:teacher
   a. purple:mauve
   b. umpire:rule
   c. chess:checkers
   d. teacher:student

[Answers: 1. b; 2. a; 3. d]

DOWNSIZE YOUR SCHOOL

Not everybody you hire works out. Some of the teachers below need to be downsized out of your school. Identify those teachers, cut them out, and throw them into the wastebasket.

Barbara Banal's class did stupendously on their standardized achievement tests. At the faculty Christmas party, Barbara offended the headmaster by calling his wife "a doofus."

Sherry Zip is a new teacher. She acquired all 30 new ESOL students this year. Sherry doesn't speak a lick of Spanish except for what she's picked up here and there ("¡Su Mama!" from her students and "¡Siente se, por favor!" from her own research). These students haven't learned a lick of English (or math, or science, or social studies) but, of course, their standardized test scores do not go on her record, they're chalked up to the ESOL teacher. The other two students in Sherry's class came in with exceptional test scores. Their test scores this year were good.

Buddy Oh covered 68 percent of his wall space this year, against fire regulations. By and large, his students did fine on the standardized tests.

Robert Uto had 32 students at the beginning of the year. He took 32 to the Museum of People of All Times and returned with 31. He took 31 to the We All Hike, We All Love Nature Walk and returned with 30. He took 30 to Everyone Can Learn and returned with 29. The trip to We All See One Another for Who We Are was canceled. All 29 kids did well on the standardized tests.

Fanny Ono can teach Computers, ESOL, Spanish, Japanese, and Dance. Fanny also called the headmaster's spouse "a doofus" at the faculty Christmas party.

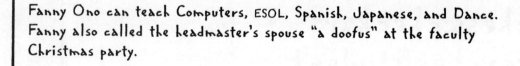

[Answer: So long, Babs and Fanny.]

WHICH ONE WAS WRITTEN BY AN ADMINISTRATOR?

Administrators have a distinct writing style. Here are three letters asking special people important questions. Can you pick out the one written by the administrator?

Darling,

I can't sleep. I can't eat. I can't breathe. I ache for you more fervently with each passing year. Will you see me again?

I am entirely yours,

Leon

Scotty:

Let's play dragons again tomorrow, OK? I think you're a really good fire-breather. Bye.

Love,

Jose

```
To:     Faculty in attendance at dinner, movie,
        and nightcap with Bob Rose on Monday,
        February 12, 1996
From:   Bob Rose
Re:     Dinner, movie and nightcap on Monday,
        February 12, 1996
```

```
    I am pleased to announce that things have gotten off
on the right foot! I am proud to say that not only did
everyone arrive on time, but those in attendance found
innovative and new things to order. It comes as no
surprise that, having taken that first step, everyone
was able to really enjoy the fruits of his or her new
and innovative orders.
    I am happy to report that the movie viewed on Monday,
February 12, 1996, by those in attendance sparked heated
        and lively debate. I would like for someone who was
        in attendance on Monday, February 12, 1996, to
        report to the rest of the faculty at our next
        faculty meeting this Tuesday, February 13, 1996,
        from 3:30 to 3:40 to provide an open forum for
        further discussion. I believe the nightcap on
        Monday, February 12, 1996, did not disappoint
        anyone in attendance. Keep up the high
        standards you have set for yourselves!
```

NO FAVORITES

We know it's difficult not to have favorites. But the sooner you start making a real effort to give everyone in your class equal attention, the better off you'll be. Here's a warm-up exercise: Try making eye contact with every child in this class as you read a story out loud to them. Any story will do.

CONFLICT RESOLUTION

Everyone wants his or her classroom to be like a close-knit community. In order to maintain a happy, peaceful classroom environment, you need to be able to help students resolve conflicts. Identify the viable resolutions in this picture.

WHICH WAY TO THE CLASSROOM?

This is Martha Laguna's first day as a new teacher. She's in a terrible tizzy because she can't find her classroom. Can you help Martha?

DRESS YOUR CLASSROOM FOR PARENT CONFERENCES

Parent conferences are coming up soon and you've got to get your room in shape. Place the items below in their appropriate places in the picture. Hurry, because you have only fifteen minutes before they start to arrive.

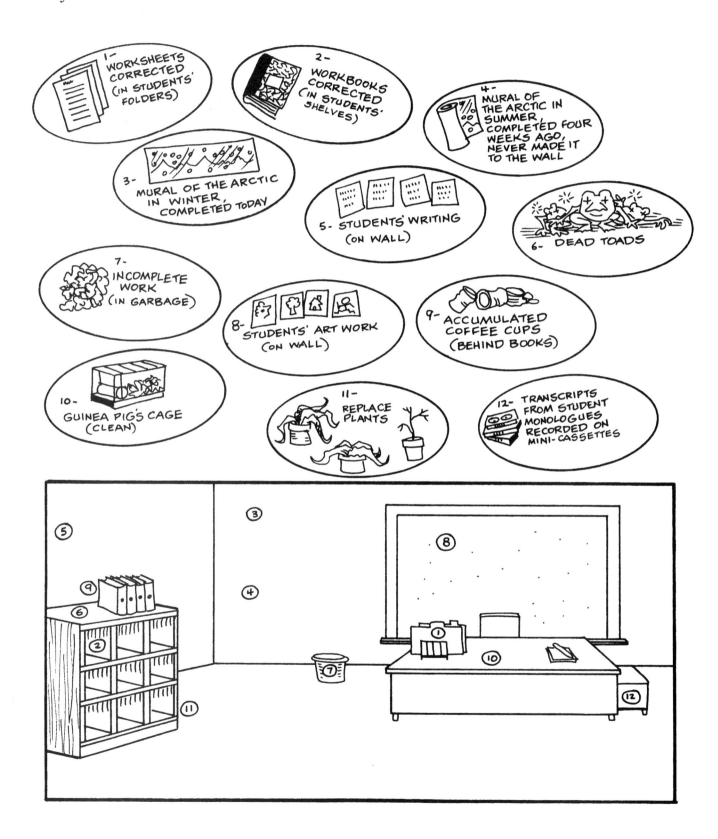

TEACHER POETRY

If you're going to teach kids how to write, you really ought to try writing yourself so that you will know your students' trials and tribulations firsthand. Complete the following poems with the words at the right to prove you've lived the writer's life.

Roses are red
Violets are blue
Teachers are writers
So what's it to _____ ?

gas

salary

noses to brown

you

noses to brown

outgrabe

There was a young lady from Bass
Who plied all her trades in the class.
Though she knew how to teach,
Discipline was a reach,
So school for kids was a _____ .

I think that I shall never see
A poem cheap as a
teacher's _____ .

'Twas brillig, and the slithy toves
Did gyre and gimble in the wabe:
All mimsy were the borogoves,
And the mome raths _____ .

The woods are lovely, dark and deep
But I have faculty meetings to keep
And _____ before I sleep
And _____ before I sleep

REJECTION CAN BE FUN!

Many young people will be looking for jobs at your school, but you won't have the money to hire them. Write a rejection letter to a graduate student in education using the following phrases:

do drop me a line once in a while . . .

so many qualified applicants . . .

four out of five dentists . . .

a penny saved is a penny earned . . .

fish out of water . . .

your outstanding record . . .

don't cry over spilt milk . . .

good luck in life . . .

wish it were otherwise . . .

HARD DAY

Hard day at work? Encounter an ungrateful student? An inconsiderate colleague? An irate parent? An unsympathetic administrator? Cut out this teddy bear. He'll comfort you. And tomorrow you'll knock 'em dead at Unfriendly Elementary.

FIND THE ACCIDENTS WAITING TO HAPPEN

As a teacher, you need to be able to anticipate accidents. X the dangerous spots in this picture and eliminate the accident before it happens.

AUDIOVISUAL 101

Teachers cannot hide the fact that they are audiovisual dunces. Here's a little help so that next time you plan to show a video, you might actually be able to do it (no guarantees).

1. Pop the tape (video) in.
2. Make sure it's rewound (press rewind button).
3. Turn on the TV (you may need help with this—you either *press* a button or *turn* a knob located on the TV itself).
4. Press play on VCR (located on the VCR itself).

Now—why is it that the darn thing still won't work?

[Answer: It's not plugged in.]

VERY SIMPLE CROSSWORD PUZZLE

Kindergarten teachers and some other teachers rejoice in the simple yet monumental accomplishments of their students. Here's an opportunity for you to take some joy in your own simple yet monumental accomplishments (hold the monumental).

Across

1. first letter in the alphabet
2. something that buzzes
4. first word in *The Teacher's Big Book of Fun*

Down

1. first letter in the alphabet
2. second letter in alphabet
3. what you do with food

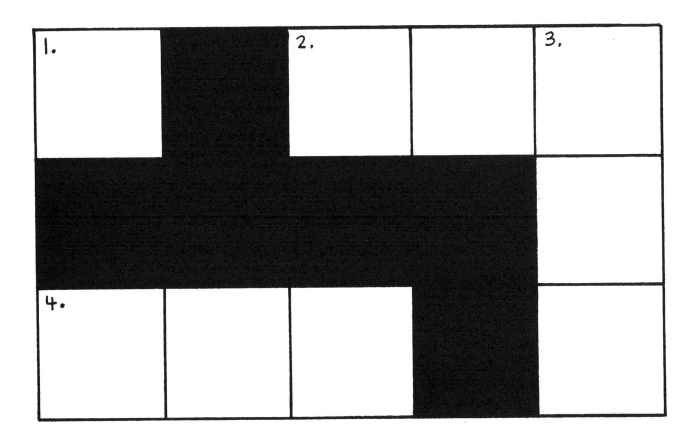

HIRING THE BEST

To attract the best teachers, you have to know how to sell your school. Practice saying these phrases with gusto:

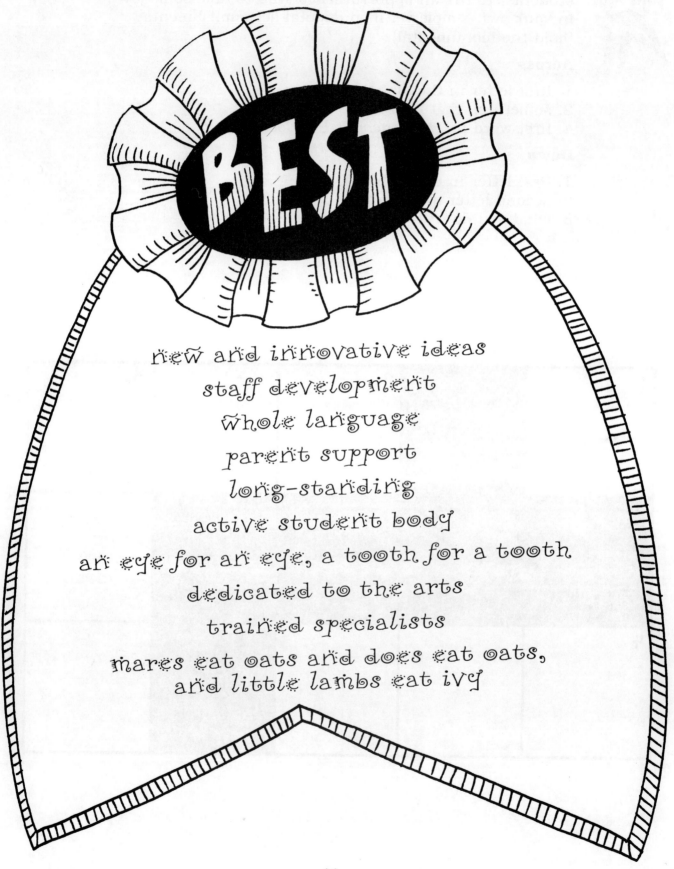

new and innovative ideas

staff development

whole language

parent support

long-standing

active student body

an eye for an eye, a tooth for a tooth

dedicated to the arts

trained specialists

mares eat oats and does eat oats,
and little lambs eat ivy

ATTACHÉ PUZZLE

It's one thing to have everything you need to look teacherly. But where do you put it all? Which of these items would you put into your attaché? Make sure the attaché closes!

HOTEL OBSTACLE COURSE

Don't let being cooped up in a stuffy hotel room during a conference be an obstacle to fun! Time yourself over courses such as this one:

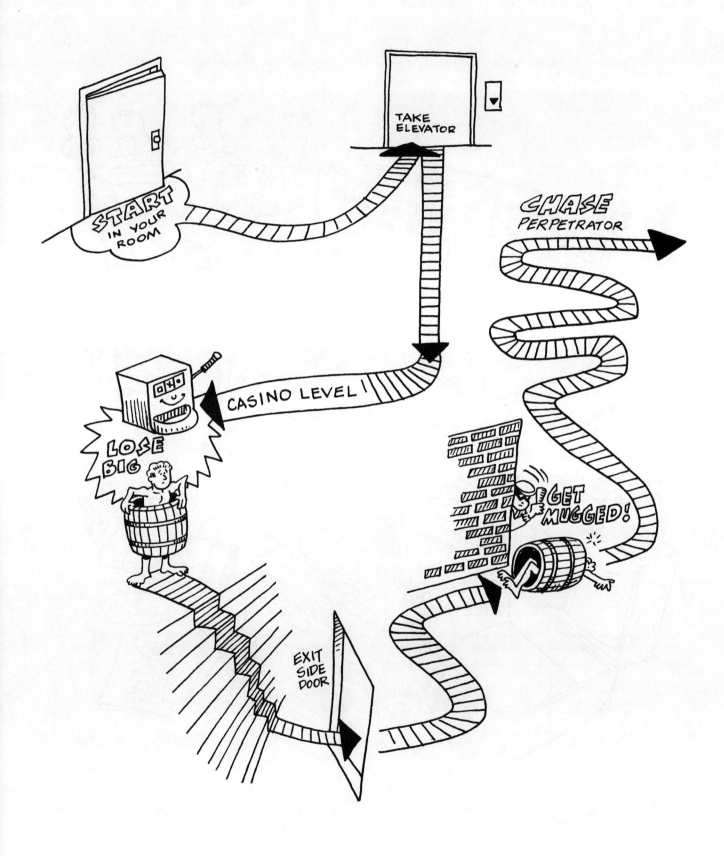

WHO'S THE FUTURE TEACHER?

Early on, kids show natural aptitudes for certain professions. Future architects build sandcastles, future soldiers play GI Joe, future lawyers carry briefcases, and future senators play doctor. Can you pick out the future teacher in this nursery school classroom?

NIGHTMARE PARENT CONFERENCE

Play this one with a friend. Here's how: Ask your friend to give you a word of the type listed next to the first blank. (Don't read the sentence—just ask for a word.) Fill in the answer. Keep going until you've completed the whole story. Then read it out loud. (Your friend *should* laugh. If he or she starts to cry, explain that the story is made up and that you doubt this will ever happen to your friend or to anyone he or she loves.)

The _____ (last name of student)s were so furious that their _____ (body part)s were trembling. They weren't going to beat around the _____ (noun). "You listen to me, you little _____ (derogatory name)!" said Mrs. _____ (insert last name). "Sit down, _____ (pet name). I'll take care of this," said Mr. _____ (insert last name). "You listen to me, you little _____ (derogatory name). _____ (first name of same student) tells us you put him/her in the _____ (adjective) reading group and the _____ (adjective) math group and that you just _____ (verb, past tense) when _____ (name of another student) _____ (verb, past tense) at him/her because, as you put it, _____ (name of student #1) is a _____ (adjective) _____ (derogatory name) and _____ (name of student #2), who we understand made it to the _____ (adjective) reading group and the _____ (adjective) math group, would never do anything wrong because s/he's a _____ (adjective) _____ (noun). Well, we've had it up to our _____ (body part)s with you and your _____ (adjective) ideas! Your _____ (body part) is _____ (word that rhymes with body part)! We're going straight from here to _____ (place)! Good day!"

PLAYING THE NUMBERS

Using the color code, paint the picture below.

Color code:
1—white
2—black
3—puce
4—vermilion
5—okra

PAPER-CLIP SHUFFLEBOARD

The object of this game is to flip the paper clip with your index
finger from the place indicated into the target. Each player receives
four paper clips per chucker. Six chuckers constitute a game. Your
score is determined by where the narrow end of the paper clip lands.
Players may try to knock other players out of the target area. Players
alternate going first. This is a game requiring little athletic ability or
brains and is thus a favorite of school administrators.

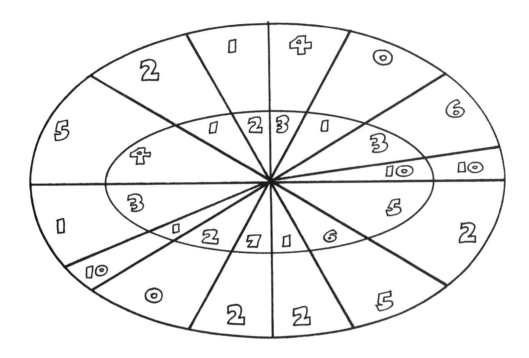

WHITE-OUT EVIL

A lot of evil forces are after teachers these days. Even nonparanoid teachers think so. Fortunately there is a weapon available to fight those evil forces—White-Out. Take your bottle of White-Out and eliminate the evil that threatens the teachers in this picture.

PLANNING FOR RETIREMENT

You certainly don't want to be a teacher forever, do you? You'd rather move someplace warm and live on the beach. But just how long will you have to work to guarantee comfortable retirement? Use the worksheet to calculate when you can retire.

PLANNING FOR RETIREMENT ☺

1. Age at which you plan to die. _____

2. Subtract age at which you plan to retire. _____

3. Number of years you will spend in retirement. _____

4. Current expenses per year × 390 percent (adjusted for inflation). _____

5. Amount you'll need for retirement (multiply line 3 by line 4). _____

6. Subtract current assets. _____

7. Add current liabilities. _____

8. Add $2 million for unexpected expenses. _____

9. Add amount of alimony you will have to pay your spouse. _____

10. Subtract Social Security payments anticipated. _____

11. Add Social Security payments anticipated (by the time you retire there won't be any Social Security). _____

12. Subtract your projected savings (not less than zero) per year from now until retirement × number of years between now and retirement. _____

13. Number of years you must work until retirement. _____

[Answer: Forget it—you're going to die with your boots on.]

75

FIND THE TEACHER

An important part of your success as a teacher is being able to deal with other teachers. To do that, you've first got to identify them. See if you can pick out the teacher in the accompanying picture.

WHAT'S WRONG WITH THIS PICTURE?

Can you find thirteen things wrong with this classroom picture?

77

TELEPHONE

Some days you just feel like saying, "Hey, I'm outta here!" You're tired, sick, or fed up. But in order to leave your students, you need a really good excuse. Well, stop your worrying. Color the message slips pink, fill in your name, and visit your nearest administrator's secretary. With slip in hand, look puzzled and distraught, and say, "Did you take this message?" (That's your exit line.)

While You Were Out
Important Message for ____

date ____ time ____

MOTHER CALLED FROM THE HOSPITAL!

While You Were Out
Important Message for ____

date ____ time ____

Neighbor called. Has something to tell you about your puppy. Thinks she should tell you face to face.

While You Were Out
Important Message for ____

date ____ time ____

SON HAS LICE. WAITING FOR YOU IN NURSES OFFICE.

While You Were Out
Important Message for ____

date ____ time ____

PAUL FROM BOARD OF ED. CAN YOU BE AT MEETING TODAY AT 11:30? BOARD WANTS TO HEAR PRESENTATION ON SCHOOLS NEED MORE FUNDING RE: GRANT MONEY!

TEACHER TRADING CARDS

Why are there trading cards for third-rate shortstops and not first-rate teachers? Cut out these cards and trade them with your friends.

Teacher of: Physical Education

Average number of soccer balls stuck in rafters per year: 2

Committees served: Picking Fair: Training Little Captains (T.L.C.); Dodge Ball: Leveling the Playing Field

Favorite colors: Black and blue

Teacher of: Kindergarten

Average number of spills at snack time/day: 2

Average number of mittens lost/year: 9

Career cases of lice: 21

Committees served: Teachers and Students Who Color; Minimizing Bathroom Breaks, Maximizing Classroom Time

Favorite colors: Yellow and orange

Teacher of: Biology

Career number of fruit flies produced in lab: 482,000,000,000

Percent blue eyed: 42

Percent brown eyed: 58

Career number of rodents escaped from lab: 6

Committees served:
Chromosomes Matter;
Teachers Against Gravity

Favorite color: Green

Average number of assemblies/year: 16

Record amount of pep at pep rallies: 739 decibels

Distinctions: Good lighting, clean bathrooms, most respectable school on field trips (by self-evaluation)

School colors: Purple and gold

NOTE TO THE SUB

You just received a message that smoke is billowing out the windows of your home. You need to leave pronto. But before you go, leave a note to the sub using this timesaving All-Purpose Substitute's Note Form.

All-purpose SUBSTITUTE'S NOTE FORM

I have been called out of the office because _____ and expect to return _____ . Keep an eye on _____ and _____ and _____ and _____ and _____ and _____ and _____ and _____ and _____ and _____ and _____ and _____ and _____ and _____ and _____ and _____ and _____ and _____ and _____ and _____ , they're really trouble.

Don't let any of them get out of their seats.

The superintendent is due to visit sometime between _____ and _____ .

Please collect all work: pages _____ thru _____ in _____ ; pages _____ thru _____ in _____ ; pages _____ thru _____ in _____ ; pages _____ thru _____ in _____ . Everyone should have plenty of time to finish everything.

Normally _____ in rm. ____ is willing to help, but it better be good.

_____ is generally trustworthy. If you have any questions, she'll probably tell you what you need to know.

If _____ and _____ start singing, you can forget about anyone doing any work. I recommend singing along (see attached lyrics).

81

LUNCH DUTY

There's nothing more degrading than having to stand there in the middle of the cafeteria screaming, "Stop that! Stop that right now! OK, that's it, the next one to throw something is going straight to . . ." while you're hit from all sides with foods from all the food groups and beyond.

Let's face it. No one can stop a really good fight. You were hired to teach! Enough is enough. Tomorrow, you go in there prepared to fight! Find the items below and pack your bag!

(OVERRIPE) TOMATOES

TOMATOES (FIRM)

MASHED POTATOES

MUSTARD

SLOPPY JOES

LIME JELLO

OLIVES BLACK AND GREEN

CATSUP

FROZEN PEAS

CHEESE

MILK

BREADS— (WHITE, RYE, AND WONDER)

SAVED BY THE BACK-UP LESSON CARDS

Imagine this. . . . You've planned to facilitate a discussion on *The Old Man and the Sea* with your sophomore English class. Roman numeral one of your outline reads, "Ask: Who finished *Old Man*?" When you ask, you are confronted with a stony silence which you take to mean that no one even started it. You deviate from your outline (i.e., Roman numeral two reads, "Ask: Who would like to open discussion?") and ask, just to be sure, "Who has started reading *The Old Man and the Sea*?" Elizabeth, a good student who rarely participates in class, raises her hand just to her shoulder. Again, you deviate from your outline and say to yourself, "Damn!" Then you remember your back-up lesson cards! You (quickly) take them out of your top desk drawer, fan 'em, and with your eyes closed, pick.

(Note: We recommend having back-up lesson cards for every lesson you attempt. Write your own on the blank cards below, cut them out, and stash them in your top desk drawer, back pocket, or left hand.)

BACK-UP LESSON CARDS

Discuss *Old Man* with Elizabeth and dismiss everyone else.

BACK-UP LESSON CARDS

Have students write essays on why they didn't do their reading and how they expect to get anywhere in life
(this generally takes 1 minute and 34 seconds— pick a back-up, back-up card).

BACK-UP LESSON CARDS

Act out *Old Man*. Characters: narrator, Old Man, boy, fishermen, father, the fish, Joe DiMaggio.

BACK-UP LESSON CARDS

Students read *Old Man* silently.

BACK-UP LESSON CARDS

Announce that you're resigning, break out Doritos, Cokes, and party hats from bottom desk drawer.

BACK-UP LESSON CARDS

Students read *Old Man* silently as you read it aloud.

BACK-UP LESSON CARDS

Have students copy "I will do my reading for English from now until the cows come home" until the bell rings.

BACK-UP LESSON CARDS

BACK-UP LESSON CARDS

BACK-UP LESSON CARDS

TEACHER ORIGAMI

Wondering what to do with all the memoranda that flood your mailbox each day? Try some teacher origami.

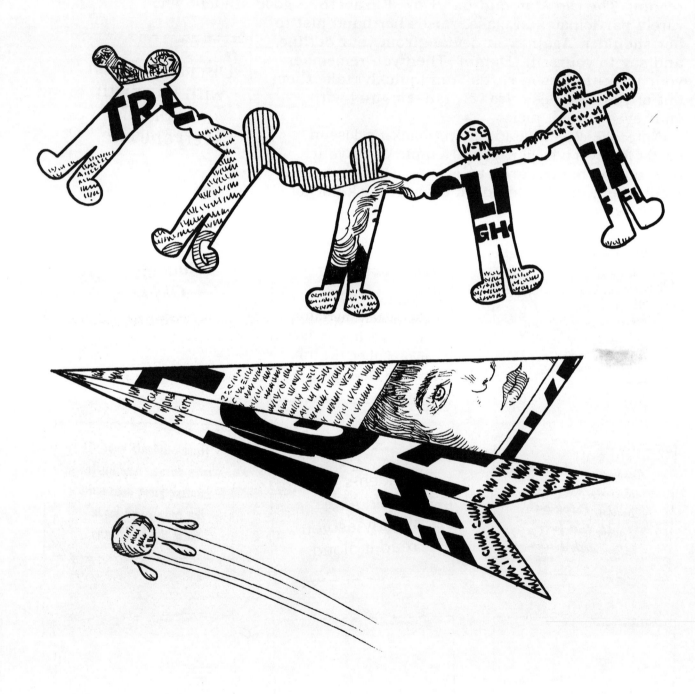

MAKE YOUR OWN MANTRA

You need a mantra for when your students, or their parents, or your colleagues, or your administrators get you down. Pick your favorite syllables from the list below and test them out, over and over and over again. If they put you at ease, really at ease, cut them out, paste them together, make several copies, and tack them up around the school as reminders.

CESS	PEE	CON
T	E	CAN
TY	AR	CAL
THREE	DRESS	LUN
THIR	MU	DANCE
ER	BREAK	CH
ING	LLAM	MEET
SHUN	SIC	HAIR
PEN	RE	SA

85

A SPECIAL SPECIAL

You and your class arrive six minutes late to art. There's a note with your name on it taped to the door. It reads: "This is the eighth time you've come strolling into my class late. According to my calculations, you've wasted a whole period of my time over the last four months. This period's on you. OFF LIMITS: GLITTER, GOOD PAINTS (KIDS KNOW WHICH), GOOD PAPER (KIDS KNOW WHICH), TISSUE PAPER, STRING, GOOD GLUE (KIDS KNOW WHICH), GOOD SCISSORS (KIDS KNOW WHICH)."

Write in the colors you'll have your class color the art teacher's walls in the areas outlined below.

THE HISTORY OF EDUCATION

It's important for you, as a teacher, to have a sense of the history of your profession and its likely future. Label these classrooms "past," "present," "future," or "post-future."

COPY FAST

Research shows that, on average, copy machines break down fourteen times per month in schools. Be prepared next time. Make thirty copies of the following page of a multiple-choice exam, by hand. Time yourself until you can make all thirty copies in one sitting.

1. How much wood could a woodchuck chuck if a woodchuck could chuck wood?

   a. about two cords
   b. a buck-and-a-half's worth
   c. enough for a roaring fire
   d. none of the above
   e. hard to say

2. As I was going to St. Ives, I met a man with seven wives, each wife had seven children, each child had seven hot dogs, and each hot dog had seven pickles. How many pickles were going to St. Ives?

   a. over 40
   b. Pickles don't go to St. Ives, silly.
   c. depends on how fast the kids ate the hot dogs
   d. none of the below
   e. The men were bigamists, so I refuse to participate in this problem as a matter of principle.

3. A plane crashed on the border between the United States and Canada. Half of the people on the plane were Canadians and the other half were from Texas. Where will they bury the survivors?

   a. none of the above
   b. depends which side of the border they land on
   c. I just got the last one, none, the pickles were going *from* St. Ives.
   d. Send everyone to Texas, there's plenty of room for them there.
   e. You don't bury the survivors.

ABOUT THE AUTHORS

Arnie Kanter is a management consultant to law firms and investment banks, a former major troublemaker in school, and the coauthor of *The Lawyer's Big Book of Fun.*

Wendy Kanter is a writer and teacher living in New York City, and the daughter and sister of the coauthors of *The Lawyer's Big Book of Fun.*

Tony Tallarico is the author and illustrator of more than 1,000 children's books, including a book for big children— *The Lawyer's Big Book of Fun.*